I Can Read

I can read.

Just listen to me.

I can read

The words I see.

green

yellow

red

cat

top

bed

All around

Are words I see,

Words to read,

Just listen to me.

Jo Ellen Moore

Getting Ready

Fill Your Room with Words

Fill your room with words. A print-rich environment is a great motivator for beginning readers. Place labels, signs, charts, and lists everywhere possible. Be sure to label the items on pages 10 and 11 so you will be ready for that activity. Provide a classroom library filled with fiction, nonfiction, and student-made books.

Variations on a Poem

Reproduce the poem on page 1 on a transparency or copy it on a chart. Read it to the class several times until students can supply some words. These variations can be used:

1. Have students recite the first stanza, then read words around the room as you point to them.
2. Substitute "I can read the numbers I see" or "I can read the letters I see."
3. Place a new list of words in the middle of the first and last stanza.

Assessment Checklist

Use the assessment checklist on page 4 to organize your observations of students.

- Check specific behaviors observed.
- Note special problems.
- Use the checklist to plan lessons in areas of need.

Parent Letter

Reproduce the parent letter on page 5. This letter explains to parents how important they are in helping their child become a successful reader. It also contains suggestions for at-home reading experiences.

Prepare Learning Centers

Learning centers allow young students to explore and experiment with information. Diverse learning styles can be met in center activities as students practice readiness\reading skills. Many of the activities in this unit can be turned into centers by putting the materials in an envelope along with simple directions.

The following types of activities are appropriate for students at the readiness/beginning reading level.

Reading centers:

Put up an ongoing center, changing activities frequently as student reading skills increase. Include some or all of the following:
- letter recognition
- sound/letter relationships
- picture/word matching
- word/sentence reading
- emergent/beginning readers

Writing centers:

Use writing centers to practice handwriting skills and to write words, sentences, or stories.
- trace and write letters
- make words using letter cards, magnetic board, letter blocks
- create sentences using word cards
- write simple stories

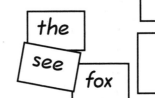

Checklist of Skills ✔

Skills								
Matches initial sounds using pictures.								
Recognizes words that rhyme.								
Matches pictures to the word they represent.								
Matches letters to their sounds.								
Recognizes own name in print.								
Recognizes classmates' names in print.								
Follows print in a book as it is read.								
Puts events of a story in order.								
Puts known words together to make a sentence.								
Recognizes common signs.								
Reads words and labels posted around the room.								
Recognizes symbols and words that give directions.								
Reads food words in text of a story.								
Writes words and sentences.								
Shows enthusiasm for reading.								
Shows enthusiasm for writing.								

Students' Names

Skills

TOM SCISSORS PENCILS

Reading Around the School EMC 562

Parent News

Dear Parents,

Your child has been learning to read letters, names, symbols, signs, and words that occur in and around our school. You can help extend your child's language and reading skills using the things that are commonly read in and around your home.

1. Read to your child frequently. This helps your child develop a large vocabulary and increases his/her knowledge and understanding. In addition, it shows your child that you think reading is important.

2. Let your child see you read frequently. The material can be books, magazines, or the newspaper. Point out the times you read for information— such as following directions when you make something, locating a word in the dictionary, or looking up a telephone number. Again, you are demonstrating that reading is important and useful.

3. Use common items and everyday events to increase your child's vocabulary.

   • Help your child read street signs and signs on buildings in your neighborhood.

   • Point to letters in magazines and newspapers. Ask your child to name the letter and give its sound.

   • Use the newspaper or magazines to help your child practice reading words. Have him/her try to find and read words being learned at school.

   • Help your child learn to read the names of the members of your family and friends.

   • Help your child read the labels on packages and containers in the kitchen.

You are the most important teacher in your child's life. Your support will help your child continue to be a successful learner.

Sincerely,

Labels and Signs

Labels Everywhere

One way to help students connect words they know to a written representation is to put labels and signs around your classroom.

1. Put student names on:
   - the children themselves
   - their personal work areas (desk, table, etc.)
   - a chart containing their pictures

2. Put signs out to identify areas of the classroom:
   - paint center
   - coat hooks
   - library corner
   - centers

3. Put labels on items around classroom:
   - bulletin board
   - chair
   - sink
   - desks
   - pencil sharpener
   - bookcase

Name It!

Reproduce pages 8 and 9. Have students cut out the cards on page 9, read the words, and then paste them to the correct item on page 8.

Pick a Star!

Reproduce the stars on pages 10 and 11. Cut the stars out and place them in a "star bag." Select one child at a time to pick a star out of the bag. The child reads the word on the star and matches it to one of the labels already placed about the room.

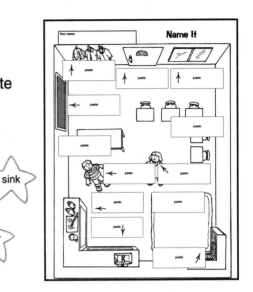

Name:

Name It

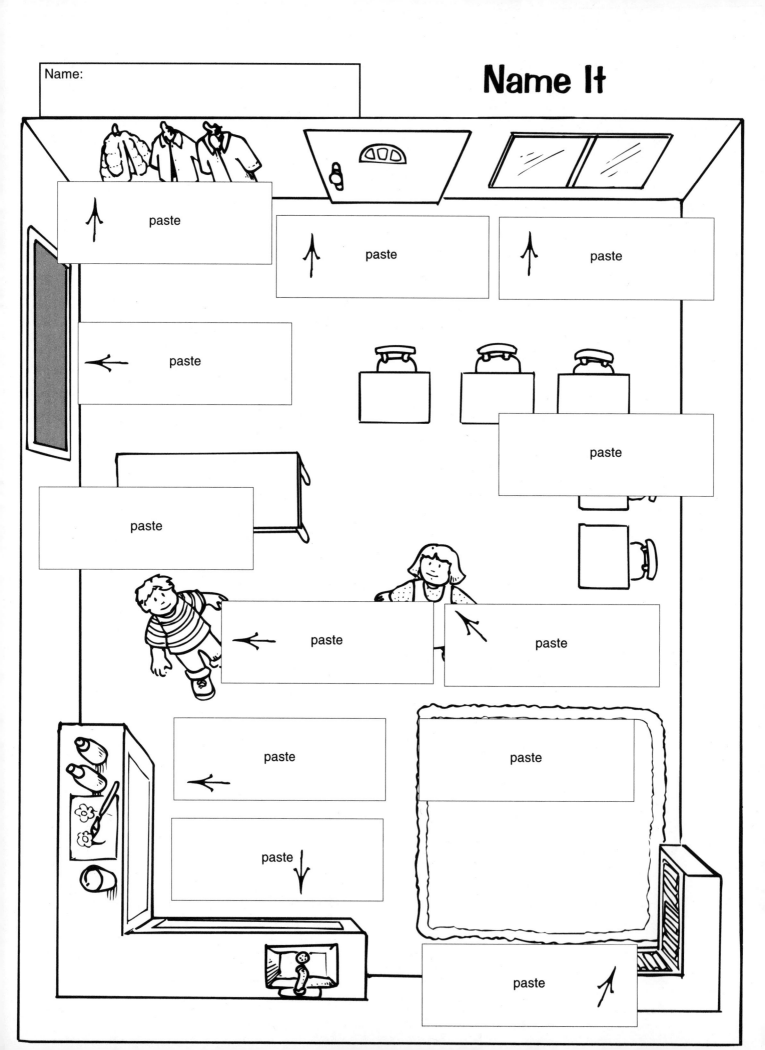

paste

Note: Reproduce this to use with *Name It!* on page 7.

Name It

1.

2.

3.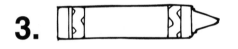

coats	desks	sink
chalkboard	boy	rug
table	girl	books
door	paint	window

paint

table

door

coats

chalkboard

paper

desks

rug

chair

books

sink

window

Charts and Lists

Songs We Sing

- Eensy Weensy Spider
- Farmer in the De[ll]
- Mary Had a Little Lamb
- Row Row Row Your Boat

Favorite Books

Strega Nona
Little White House
Sing a Song
Drummer Boy

Our Birthdays

[Jonat]hon - January 10
[Mich]elle - June 16
[Mo]rgan - December 26

Put up charts and lists for students to read. Some of these can stay up all year, while others will change as your curriculum and the seasons change.

1. Put up charts with words and pictures for units of study. For example, if you are studying animals, make a chart of animal pictures with their names and a sentence or two describing each animal and what it does.

2. Put up charts containing poems your students have learned and poems they have written.

3. Keep ongoing lists of:
   - songs they've learned
   - books you've read aloud
   - visitors to the class

4. Make a chart listing student birthdays.

Charts and lists can be made on large sheets of tagboard, chart paper, or butcher paper. Write a heading and add a decorative illustration or border. Pages 14-15 contain headings and clip art that can be reproduced for use on your charts.

Make a Class Scrapbook

Keep an ongoing class scrapbook containing photographs and text about daily class activities, special events, guests, trips, letters and other memorabilia collected for students to read. Read pages from the scrapbook periodically with your students. Place the scrapbook in the class library for everyone to read.

Materials:
- a brown paper grocery bag (with or without an attached handle)
- butcher paper
- 4 large brass paper fasteners
- copies of page headings on pages 14-15
- hole punch

Steps to follow:

1. Cut the brown paper grocery bag as shown here:

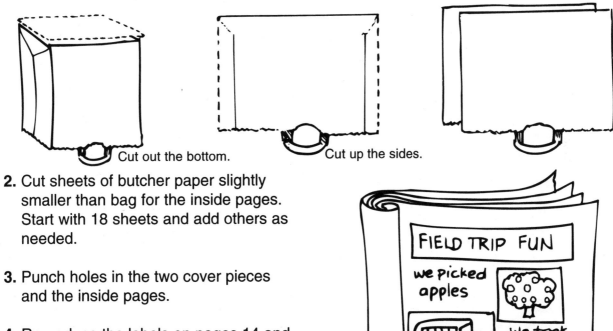

Cut out the bottom.   Cut up the sides.

2. Cut sheets of butcher paper slightly smaller than bag for the inside pages. Start with 18 sheets and add others as needed.

3. Punch holes in the two cover pieces and the inside pages.

4. Reproduce the labels on pages 14 and 15 to head various sections of the scrapbook.

5. Tape or glue pictures, photos, and other memorabilia to the inside pages. Label each item to help children remember its significance.

Note: Reproduce these to use as labels in the class scrapbook.

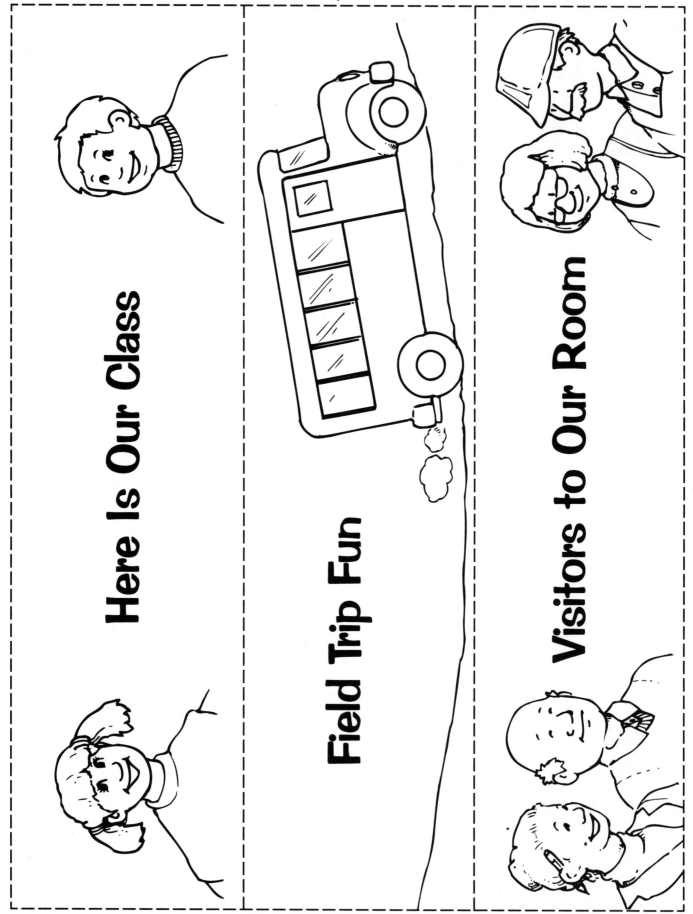

Here Is Our Class

Field Trip Fun

Visitors to Our Room

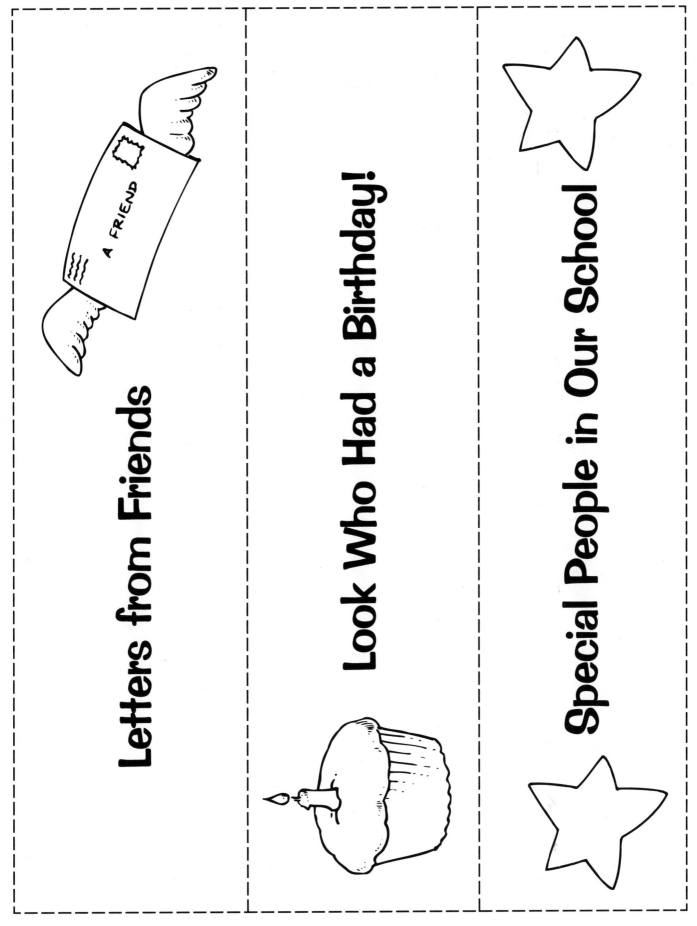

Letters from Friends

Look Who Had a Birthday!

Special People in Our School

Reading Names

One of the first words children learn to read is their own name. Using student names provides many opportunities for sound and word reading practice. Begin by labeling children's classroom belongings with name tags.

Name Tags

Reproduce the name tags on page 18 for students to wear at the beginning of the school term, whenever there is a guest speaker or other visitors to class, and on field trips.

What's My Name?

Make opportunities for students to read each other's names.

1. Listed Places

Keep lists of student names wherever possible. For example:

- on a "Class Helpers" chart
- at centers
- on a birthday chart

2. Hop Along

Make a set of tagboard squares 6" x 6" (15 x 15 cm). Write a child's name on each card. Tape the cards on the floor. The names can be arranged in a block or in a line. Have students hop from card to card, reading each name as they step on it. (Variation: name the initial letter or give the initial sound.)

3. Beginning Reader

Reproduce the beginning reader *Ben's Lost Book* on pages 56-59. Directions for making and using the book are found on page 54.

4. Pictures and Names in "Books"

Create class books containing student names. These can be logs of field trips you've taken, photo books of your students at work in the classroom, or books where children have drawn and written about themselves in the third person.

Mrs. Miller's Class on the Playground

Our Trip to the Bakery

Tony's Book

What Letter Do You See?

Use student names to practice identifying and naming letters.

1. Ask "What letter does your first name begin with?" "What letter does your last name begin with?" Explain that these are called your *initials*. Write a letter on the chalkboard and say "Stand up if this letter is the initial of your first name." Repeat until you have covered all of the initials in your classroom.

2. Write your own name on the chalkboard. Underline the first letter in each of your names with colored chalk. Remind children that these letters are called *initials*. Call up several children at a time have them write their name on the board and underline their initials. Repeat until everyone has had a turn. Ask "Does anyone in class have the same initials as you?"

3. Ask students to line up as you give the *first name* initials in ABC order. When everyone is in line, explain that they are lined up in the same order as the letters of the alphabet (alphabetical order).

4. Make a center activity by writing each person's initials and name on separate tagboard strips. Put five or more sets of names and initials in an envelope to use as a matching activity.

What Sound Do You Hear?

Have students listen for the initial sound of their names. Say a sound. Have everyone whose name begins with that sound stand up. Finally, ask each child to tell you the sound his/her name begins with.

Name Hunt

Reproduce page 19. Children are to find someone in class whose name begins with the letter/sound listed on the paper. That child writes his/her name after the letter.

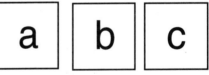

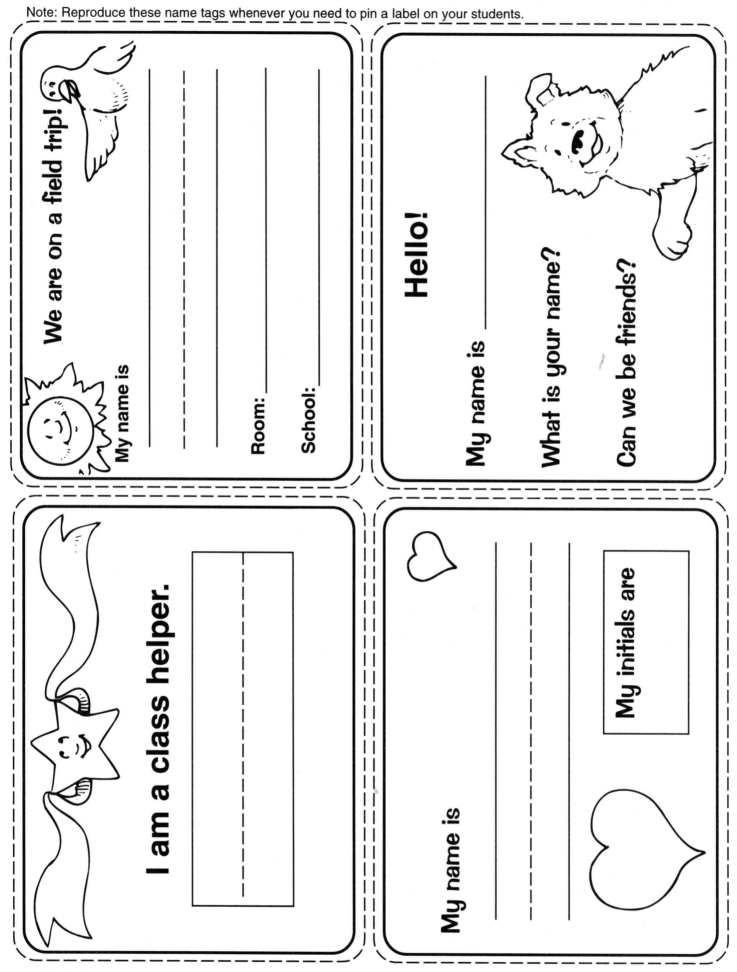

We are on a field trip!

My name is _____

Room: _____

School: _____

Hello!

My name is _____

What is your name? _____

Can we be friends? _____

I am a class helper.

My name is _____

My initials are _____

My Name Hunt

Look at the names of my friends.

B

K

S

W

T

R

C

Books to Read

Classroom Library

Provide many opportunities for students to experience books. Read to your students several times a day. Put the books, poems, and other material you read in an accessible area so children can explore them again and again.

Set up a library of fiction and nonfiction books, student-made books, and children's magazines. Put the books in categories on your library book shelves or in separate containers. Label each area or container (see labels on page 21). Encourage students to predict which section a new book has come from.

My Reading Log

Page 22 contains a reproducible reading log. Have students keep the log as they read books throughout a designated amount of time (week, month, unit of study). They are to write the title on the sheet, and evaluate the book by coloring in the appropriate picture.

You may want to assign a certain type of book to be explored (counting books, animal books, true books, etc.) or have free choice of books to read.

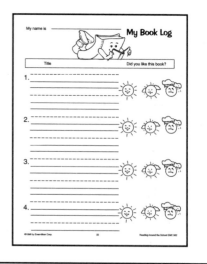

Fairy Tales

Alphabet Books

Counting Books

Picture Books

Easy-to-Read

Poetry

Song Books

Animal Books

My name is _____

My Book Log

Title	Did you like this book?

1. -
   _____
   _____
   -
   _____
   _____

2. -
   _____
   _____
   -
   _____
   _____

3. -
   _____
   _____
   -
   _____
   _____

4. -
   _____
   _____
   -
   _____

Reading Around the School EMC 562

Reading the Bulletin Board

"Things We Use" Board

Set up a bulletin board containing real things students read in their daily lives.

Cover a large bulletin board with brightly colored butcher paper. Add the title "*Things We Use.*"

Collect real items that your children may be exposed to at school or at home. Label them and pin them to the bulletin board.

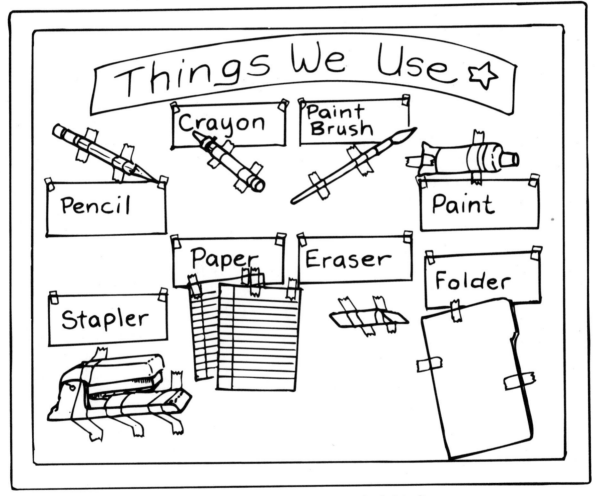

Ask students to read the name of each object as you point to it.

Repeat this over a period of time. When you think your students are ready, take down the name labels. Show each label, one at a time, and select someone to place it next to the correct item.

Any topic your class is studying can provide artifacts or pictures that can be put on a bulletin board to build speaking and reading vocabulary.

Photo Bulletin Board

Set aside a bulletin board for displaying photographs of real people around your school. Add a title "Who Am I?" List each person's name and job. Make reading this bulletin board a part of "reading the room."

Variations:

- Show photographs of your students at work in the classroom or at play outdoors. Add a sentence or two by each photo.
- Display photographs from field trips your class takes.
- Put up photographs of special people who visit your class. Add a few sentences explaining what they did on their visit.

Place the photographs in your class scrapbook when they are removed from the bulletin board.

Display Student Work

Find a place in your classroom where each child can have a special spot to display a favorite project they have worked on. Let students change their work sample whenever they have a new one to share. The samples may be saved to add to the students' portfolio of work. The students "Own Spot" may be reserved with a clothespin and an identification tag with their name on it.

Identification Tag Patterns

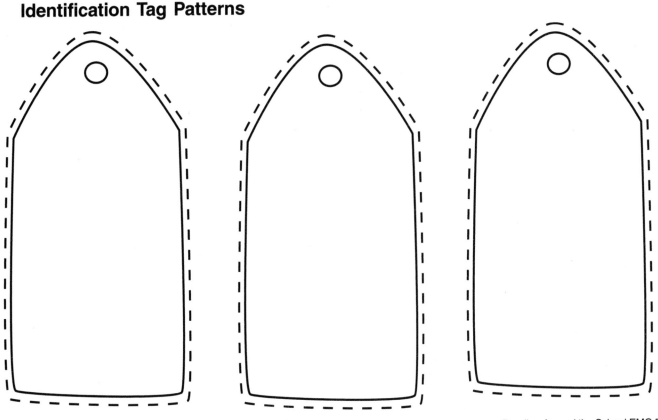

Reading the Calendar

October

Sunday	Monday	Tuesday	Wednesday	Thursday	Friday	Saturday
	1 Toms birthday	2 We painted trees today	3 We saw lightning	4 We made clay today	5 We went on a trip to the farm	6
7				11	12	13
14				18	19	20
			24	25	26	27
			31			

A Class Log

Turn your calendar into a class log and provide another opportunity to begin reading words that are a part of daily life.

How to Make:

Cut a sheet of butcher paper 30" x 35" (76 x 89 cm). Use a wide marking pen to mark off space for the name of the month, the days of the week, and the numbers (you may want to add these each day rather than have them all up at one time).

How to Use:

Each day practice reading the name of the month and the days of the week. Take time before dismissing school to have students review what happened during the day. Write important information about what happened in class. Use words and pictures your students can read as much as possible. Review the information periodically throughout the month.

During the last week of school, post all of the calendars for the year. This creates a "timeline" of what has happened in class throughout the year. Students love reminiscing about what they have done and learned.

At Home

Reproduce the calendar on page 28 each month for students to keep track of their schedule at home. Make one copy and write in the month and the dates before reproducing class copies. You may also write in any special school events (open house, parent conference, field trip, etc.) you want them to remember.

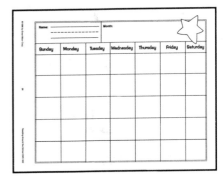

The Names of the Months

Practice the months of the year by learning the chant on page 32 and letting students solve the seasons' puzzle on page 33.

Mulberry Bush

Practice the days of the week by playing "Here we go 'round the mulberry bush."

1. Teach the version of the song shown on pages 30 and 31. Have students skip around the circle as they sing the chorus, and then stop and do the action as they sing the verses.

2. Reproduce the days of the week from page 29. Show each day in same order as in the song and have students read them with you. Mix up the cards and show one card at a time. Have the class read the word and then select someone to show you that day of the week on the class calendar. Finally, place the cards along the tray of the chalkboard. Ask students to come up and put them in the correct order.

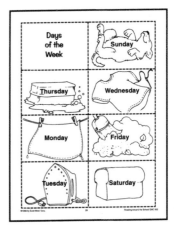

Name: _____

Month: _____

Sunday	Monday	Tuesday	Wednesday	Thursday	Friday	Saturday

Days of the Week

Sunday

Thursday

Wednesday

Monday

Friday

Tuesday

Saturday

Reading Around the School EMC 562

Mulberry Bush
A Traditional Game

Chorus:
Here we go 'round the mulberry bush,
The mulberry bush, the mulberry bush.
Here we go 'round the mulberry bush,
So early in the morning.

This is the way we wash our clothes,
Wash our clothes, wash our clothes.
This is the way we wash our clothes,
So early **Monday** morning.

This is the way we iron our clothes,
Iron our clothes, iron our clothes.
This is the way we iron our clothes,
So early **Tuesday** morning.

This is the way we mend our clothes,
Mend our clothes, mend our clothes.
This is the way we mend our clothes,
So early **Wednesday** morning.

This is the way we scrub the floor,
Scrub the floor, scrub the floor.
This is the way we scrub the floor,
So early **Thursday** morning.

This is the way we sweep the house,
Sweep the house, sweep the house.
This is the way we sweep the house,
So early **Friday** morning.

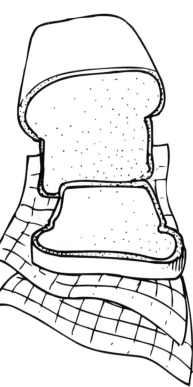

This is the way we bake our bread,
Bake our bread, bake our bread.
This is the way we bake our bread,
So early **Saturday** morning.

This is the way we take our rest,
Take our rest, take our rest.
This is the way we take our rest,
So early **Sunday** morning.

One Year

January,

February,

March,

The months go passing by.

April,

May,

June,

I can't stop them if I try.

July,

August,

September,

I really wonder why?

October,

November,

December,

My, how the year does fly!

J. E. Moore

The Seasons of the Year

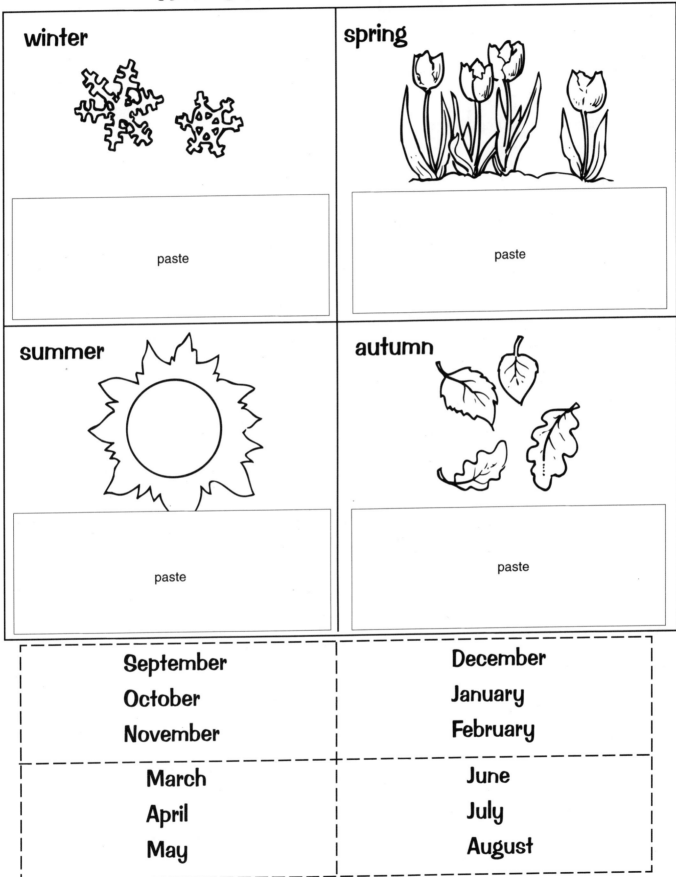

winter

paste

spring

paste

summer

paste

autumn

paste

September	December
October	January
November	February
March	June
April	July
May	August

Reading Around the School EMC 562

Words and Symbols Tell Us What to Do

Teach students the symbols and words you use to represent items and directions on activity sheets and center direction charts.

1. Make a set of cards using the symbols on page 35. Gather the same real items. Place the cards where students can see them. Show a pair of scissors. Ask students what scissors are used for (to cut). Ask them to decide which card shows the symbol for "cut." Select a child to pick up the card (scissor symbol) and place it by the scissors. Repeat until each card and real item are matched.

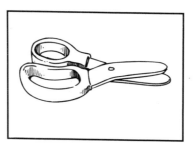

2. Use this activity for students ready to move from picture symbols to words. Reproduce the word cards on page 36. Show each word card to your students and place it next to the symbol it names. Point out the initial sounds and length of the words as ways to help students remember the words. Mix up the cards and pass them out to students. Have children find the person with the card that matches theirs to make a set containing the picture symbol and the function word.

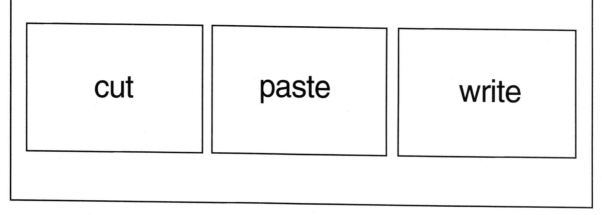

| cut | paste | write |

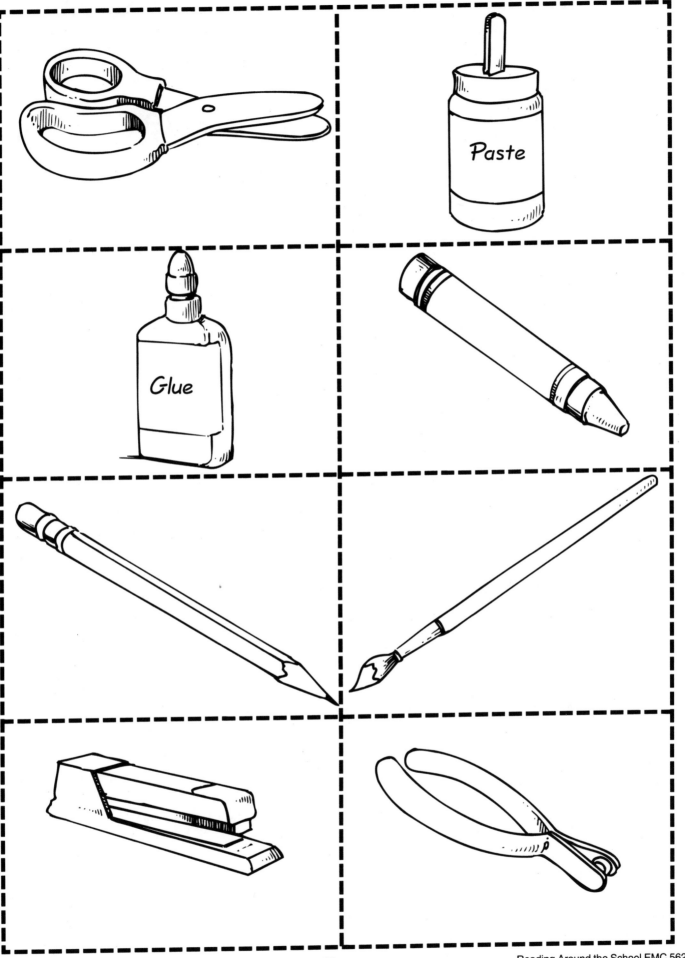

Paste

Glue

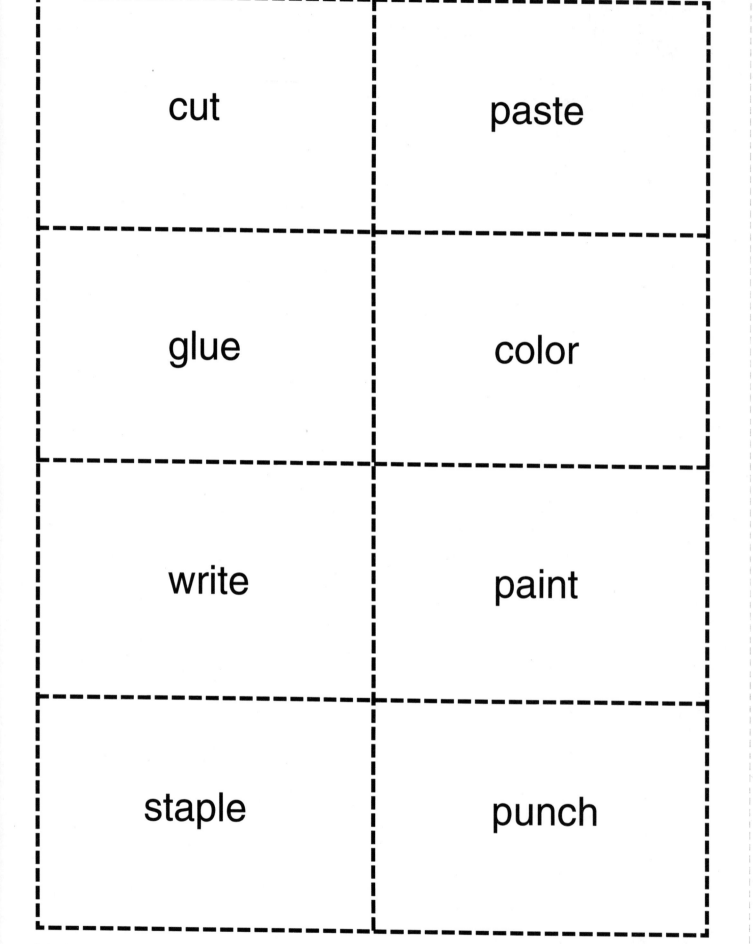

cut

paste

glue

color

write

paint

staple

punch

Everyday Symbols Pop-Up Book

Everyone loves reading a pop-up book. This activity will allow students to gain further practice in reading words that represent symbols they see every day. These books are best made in small groups with the directions being given at each step.

Materials:
- a pop-up form (page 38)
- a cover form (page 39)
- copies of the symbol cards (pages 35-36)
- crayons, scissors, and paste

Steps to follow:
1. Cut and fold the pop-up form as shown.

2. Have each child choose one symbol card from page 35 and the matching word card from page 36.

3. Put paste on the front of each tab on the pop-up book. Affix the matching symbol cards on the tabs.

4. Write a phrase or sentence on the line.

5. Color the background to show something about the sentence.

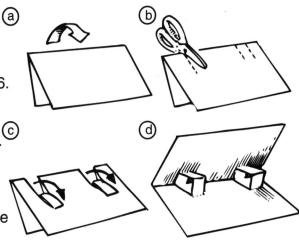

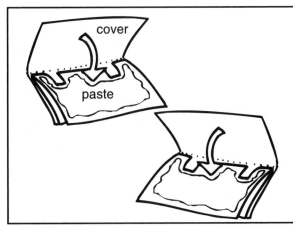

Put the pop-up in the cover:

Fold the cover form, and place closed pop-up form inside.

Smear paste on the top of the pop-up.

Close the cover and press.

Flip the book over and repeat the process.

Color the cover to show something about the sentence.

               Reading Around the School EMC 562

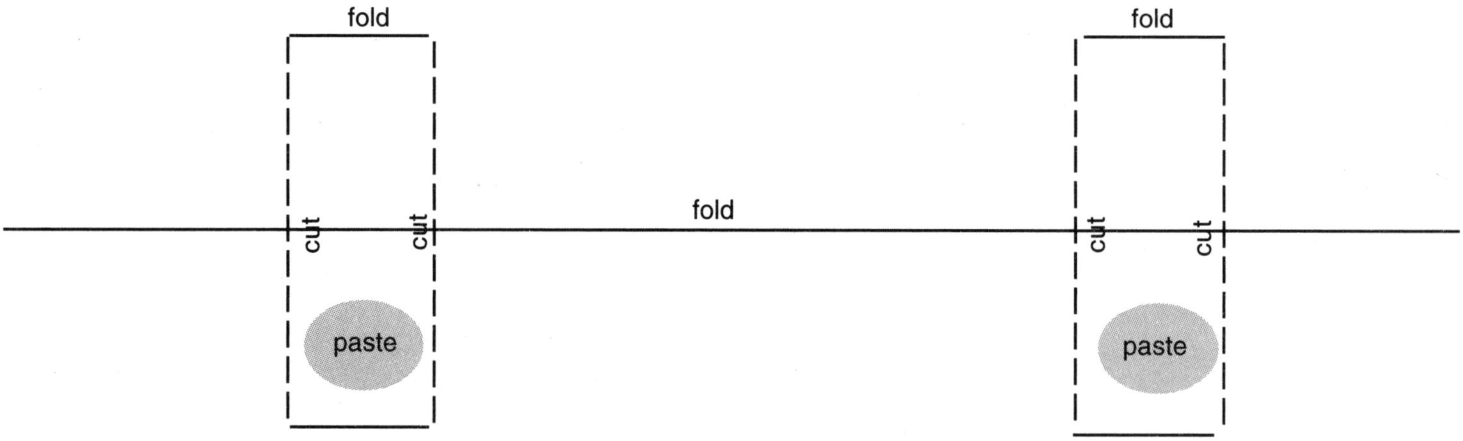

fold

fold

fold

cut

cut

cut

cut

paste

paste

The End

---
fold

Words I Use

_____

_ _ _ _ _ _ _ _ _ _ _ _ _ _ _ _ _ _ _

_____
Name

Words Around Our School

We're Going on a Word Hunt

Remind your students that words are everywhere and that they are important because they give us information. Explain that they are going to be detectives out to "capture" words. Decide in advance whether they can simply find a word or if they must "read" the word in order to "capture" it.

Word Hunt

Office	Supply Room
Foothill School	Winston Street
Bus 33	Room 16
boys	girls
Library	Cafeteria

1. Reproduce the pattern on page 41 to make "spy glasses" for students to use as they "hunt" for words.
   - Cut out the pattern from tagboard. Leave the opening empty or use plastic laminate scraps as "glass."
   - Tape the laminate to one side of the spyglass.
   - Fold the two sides together.
   - Tape the "spy glass" to a tongue depressor handle. (This is a good project for an eager parent volunteer or an older student.)

2. Walk around the school and neighborhood. When a word is discovered, let someone read it. Write down any words the children "capture." When you return to class, write these words on a chart. Post the chart with a "spyglass" for children to use as they "read the room."

Our School

Reproduce the school map on page 42. This maze asks students to begin at the office and find the library by drawing a line and moving through the maze. Have students read the words they pass.

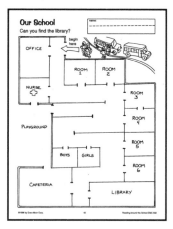

Around Our School—A Book

Provide students with the the forms on page 43-45. Each student will need four of the writing forms on page 44, one cover form on page 43 and one picture form on page 45.

1. Students cut out and paste one picture in each box.

2. They circle the name of the area shown and write the word on the blank line.

This little book gives the opportunity to review school location words that you want the students to learn to read.

Spyglass Pattern

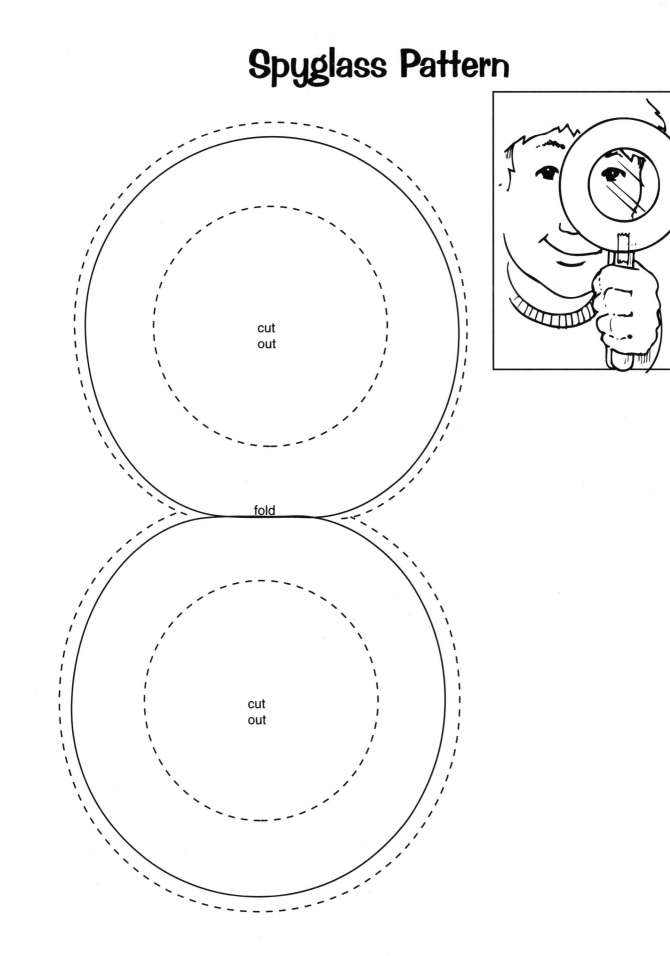

cut
out

fold

cut
out

Our School

Can you find the library?

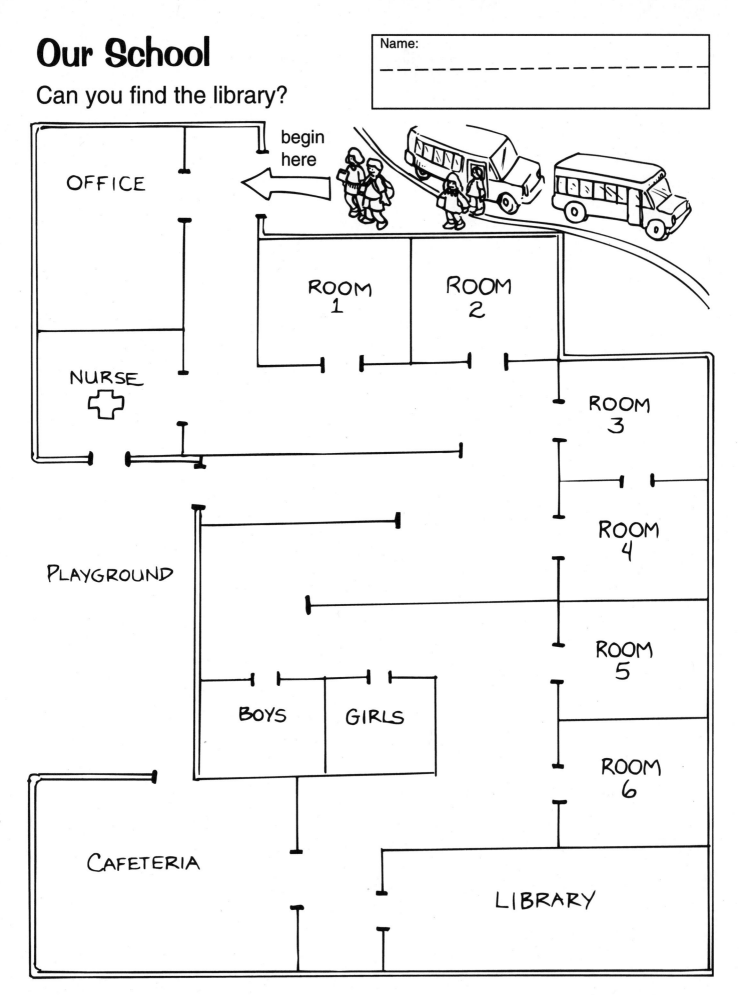

begin here

OFFICE

NURSE

ROOM 1

ROOM 2

ROOM 3

ROOM 4

ROOM 5

ROOM 6

PLAYGROUND

BOYS

GIRLS

CAFETERIA

LIBRARY

Reading Around the School EMC 562

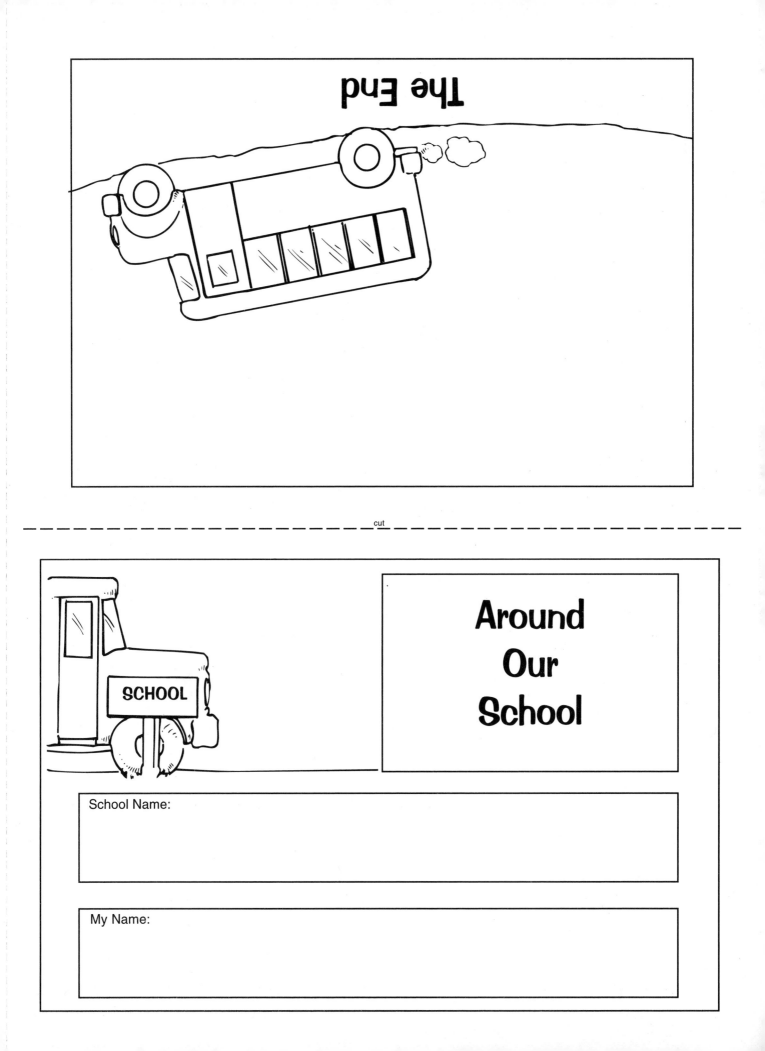

The End

- - - - - - - - - - - - - - cut - - - - - - - - - - - - - -

Around
Our
School

SCHOOL

School Name:

My Name:

Circle one:

office

bus

boys bathroom

girls bathroom

library

playground

cafeteria

nurse

ABC

I can find the _____ in my school.

Circle one:

office

bus

boys bathroom

girls bathroom

library

playground

cafeteria

nurse

ABC

I can find the _____ in my school.

boys

girls

LIBRARY

CAFETERIA

NURSE

What Does the Sign Say?

Signs and symbols are valuable "words" for children to learn to read. They are found everywhere and provide important information.

Reproduce the cards on page 47- 49. (Enlarge them or make transparencies if you are working with a large class.) Show each sign and ask "What does this sign tell you?" Teach any of the words or symbols that are unfamiliar to your students.

Practice the words in one or more of the following ways:

- Mix up the cards. Show them one at a time and have the class read the word. Show them again and choose individuals to read each card.

- Play "Stop-Go/Walk-Don't Walk." Make large copies of the words *stop, go, walk*, and *don't walk*. Have children line up across the end of the playground facing you. Show the cards in random order. Students walk when they see "Go" or "Walk" and stop when they see "Stop" or "Don't Walk."

Note: Reproduce these signs to use with the activities on page 46.

Note: Reproduce these signs to use with the activities on page 46.

GREEN STREET

FIRE
EXTINGUISHER

DANGER

DO NOT
ENTER

In the Cafeteria

What's for Lunch

Take advantage of lunch or snack time to practice reading skills.

1. Reproduce the form on page 51 and write the day's cafeteria menu on it. Make word cards for each item. Read the menu with your students. Then show each word card. Have students read the cards with you. Pass the cards out. Have students match the cards to the chart.

Make a list on the chalkboard of foods in lunches brought from home. If you have children who go home for lunch, add what they ate to the list when they return to school.

Read the cafeteria menu and the words on the chalkboard to review all the different types of foods eaten for lunch that day.

2. Discuss lunch favorites with your students. Pass out sheets of drawing paper and have each child draw a picture of his/her favorite lunch. Help them to label the foods in their pictures.

3. Reproduce the beginning reader "What's For Lunch?" on pages 61-64 for reading practice. Teaching ideas for using the reader can be found on pages 54-55.

Lunch Lotto

Lunch Lotto is played with 4 players. Each player needs a *Lunch Lotto* gameboard (page 52). Make 4 copies of the picture cards on page 53. The cards are cut apart, shuffled, and placed face down in the center of the players.

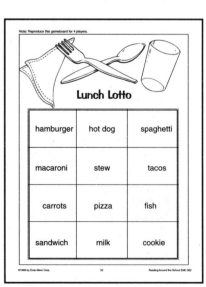

Each player in turn draws a card, reads the name, and places the card on the matching spot of their gameboard. If a player draws a duplicate card, it is placed in a discard pile.

The first player to cover all of the boxes is the winner.

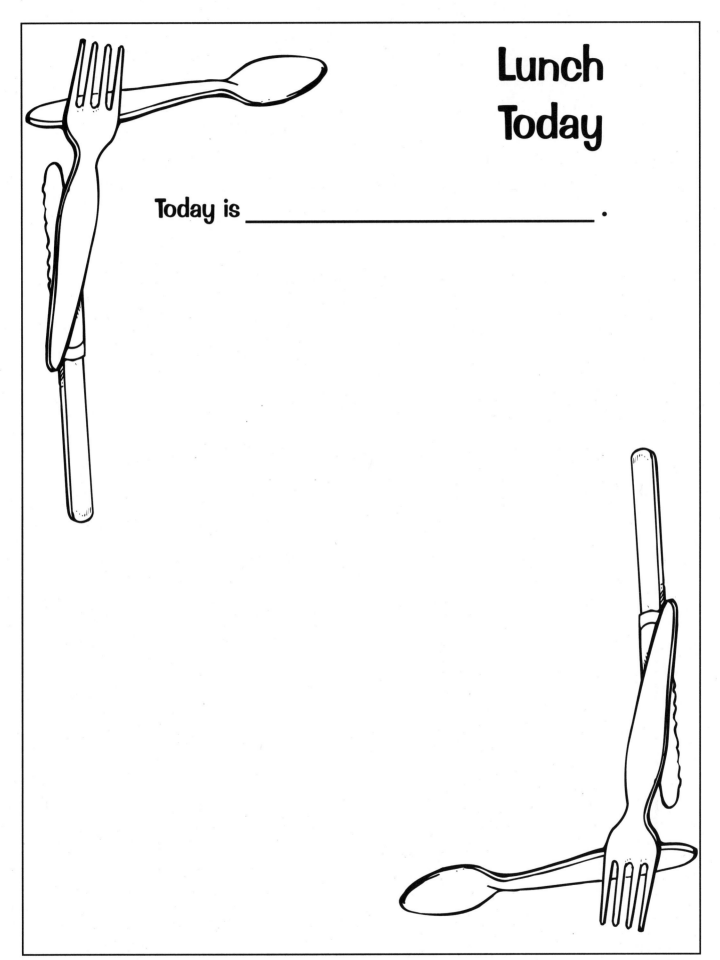

Lunch Today

Today is _____ .

Lunch Lotto

hamburger	hot dog	spaghetti
macaroni	stew	tacos
carrots	pizza	fish
sandwich	milk	cookie

Note: Make four sets of these picture cards to use with the activity on page 50.

Lunch Lotto Playing Cards

hamburger	hot dog	spaghetti
macaroni	stew	tacos
carrots	pizza	fish
sandwich	milk	cookie

Reproducible
Beginning Readers

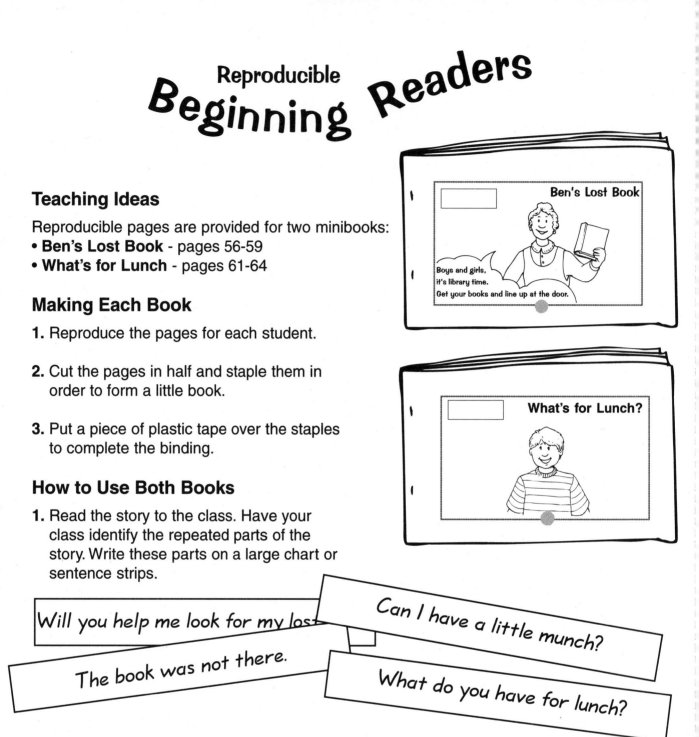

Teaching Ideas

Reproducible pages are provided for two minibooks:
- **Ben's Lost Book** - pages 56-59
- **What's for Lunch** - pages 61-64

Making Each Book

1. Reproduce the pages for each student.

2. Cut the pages in half and staple them in order to form a little book.

3. Put a piece of plastic tape over the staples to complete the binding.

How to Use Both Books

1. Read the story to the class. Have your class identify the repeated parts of the story. Write these parts on a large chart or sentence strips.

Will you help me look for my los[t]

Can I have a little munch?

The book was not there.

What do you have for lunch?

2. Read the story again, having the whole class read the repeated words when you point to them. Write each word of the repeated story parts on a tagboard card. Pass the words out and have students read their word and find it on the chart.

3. Write each line of the story on sentence strips. Place these in a sentence holder or pin to a bulletin board. Have the class "read" the story with you as you point to each line. Pass out the sentences and have students place them in the correct order. Allow students to help each other read the lines if necessary.

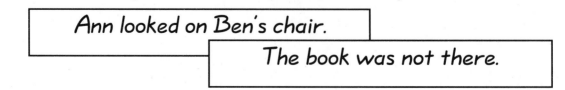

Ann looked on Ben's chair.

The book was not there.

4. Reproduce the word cards on pages 60 and the inside back cover. Give each student the words for one of the sentences. Have students read their cards and match them to the same words in their own books.

Have students arrange the words to make their sentence. Move around the room to check the sentence order.

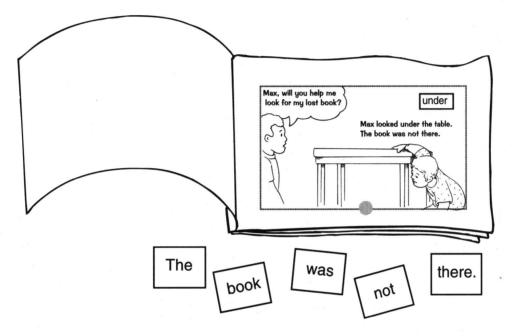

5. Read the story to your class as they follow along in their books. (Let them read along on the sentences they know.) At the end of each page, ask, "What two words do you hear that rhyme (sound the same)?" At the end of the story write the rhyming words on the chalkboard. Ask, "Can you tell me any other words that rhyme with *(look and book) (lunch and munch)*?" List these words on a chart. Have the class read the completed chart with you.

---

on • in • under • over

Ben's Lost Book contains several positional words. After reading each page, ask students to tell you where the children in the story looked for the book. Hand a book to a student. Ask him/her to place the book in a specific position. ("Put the book in the ball box." "Put the book behind my desk.") Write the positional words on the chalkboard. Point to each word and read it with your class.

My Book

Name_____

Ben's Lost Book

Boys and girls.
It's library time.
Get your books and line up at the door.

1

Ben looked and looked.
He couldn't find his book.

2

on

Ann, will you help me look for my lost book?

Ann looked on Ben's chair. The book was not there.

3

in

Lee, will you help me look for my lost book?

Lee looked in Ben's desk. The book was not there.

4

Sam, will you help me look for my lost book?

in

Sam looked in Ben's lunch bag.
The book was there!

7

Thank you all for helping me look.
Now I have my library book.

8

Ben's Lost Book
Word Cards

look	for	my
Will	you	help
book?	me	lost
The	book	was
not	there.	

60

My Book

Name_____

What's for Lunch?

1

I am so hungry.

I can't wait.

What's for lunch today?

Let's not be late.

2

Can I have a little munch?

7

I had a bite of sandwich and a sip of juice.

I had a bite of burrito with beans and cheese.

I had a bite of yogurt and fruit.

I had a bite of chicken and a carrot stick.

I had a sip of soup and a bite of apple.

I'm not hungry anymore!

8